# Compulsion

## Pat Grieco

**Other Books by Pat Grieco**

The Art of Nauga Farming

Rhetoric

The Book of Light

Print ISBN: 978-1-7324688-4-9
Pen and Lute
www.penandlute.com

The final approval for this literary material is granted by the
author.

Library of Congress Control Number: 2018956657

Distributed Publication
Lexington, KY
Middletown, DE
San Bernardino. CA

# DEDICATION

**For those who hear the unspoken**

# Compulsion

## Pat Grieco

Grieco

They call, and I must follow

# Contents

Wind ..............................................................1

Soft into the night ..........................................2

A new pup.......................................................3

I almost lived ................................................5

Come to me ....................................................7

A Name..........................................................10

At first sight ................................................14

A Word ..........................................................17

The Legend of the Fire Tree ...........................19

Bespoken.......................................................21

A Caged Bird ................................................25

The birth of the new world ...........................28

Consequences ...............................................30

Corruption.....................................................34

One last hope ................................................38

Future Tense ................................................40

Speak Truth to Power ....................................44

An Autumn's Walk........................................47

All tomorrows...............................................50

Compulsion...................................................51

Another You ................................................53

The middle ...................................................55

A wondrous thing .........................................58

A veteran's salute .........................................60

This face.......................................................62

Changeling......................................................................65

Tom Bailey .....................................................................66

Consumed ......................................................................69

You could see it in his face...........................................71

Denial.............................................................................75

Early Frost .....................................................................77

Escape ............................................................................79

A Winter's Walk.............................................................82

By the time I leave .........................................................85

But one thing..................................................................89

A path beneath the river................................................92

When next I wake ...........................................................94

As Seen Through Amber .................................................96

But one day more............................................................100

Flood ..............................................................................102

# Wind

One cannot change the wind by wishing.
It does not respect our desires.
It does not heed our needs.
It will not shift or turn
because we want it so.

It simply is.
A fact made more so by ignoring it.
A fact that governs nothing.
For we need not go where the wind blows.
We can stand or move against it.
We can travel where our will drives us.

We can do so blithely
with no regard for breeze or gale
but the wind still blows,
it still pushes and buffets,
hinders or helps,
depending on the course we set.

We may fight against it
or ride it to our destination,
but we cannot change it.
It simply is.

# Soft into the night

Soft into the night we go
with no remembrance of the day.
Was it bright?
Was there ever such a thing as sun
which filled the sky with light
and set the world aglow?

Blue,
that most amiable of colors,
becomes muted and dim
as shadows capture all
and even scattered bits of light,
lingering upon the heights,
flee the encroaching dark.

Only palest moon adorns the sky
with nothing of itself
to give the land below.

The land in turn sits silent
in the absence of its truest love
to shiver 'neath night's mantle
fearing sun might never come again.

But grant a glimmer,
the slightest hint
that light and warmth shall reappear
and all will rest content within this night
'til faith should make it so
and day with sun be born again.

## A new pup

Nothing
makes you feel so old
as a new pup.
All the energy and movement,
the demands and training,
the early mornings
and the constant cleaning
after piles or pools are found.

It's tiring.
It's exasperating.
It tests one's patience
and endurance
while the pup
and you
both learn.

Nothing
makes you feel so young
as a new pup.
All the energy and movement,
the tireless approach
to each new thing,
every leaf a taste sensation,
every stick a toy to chew,
every stone a treasure
to push and prod and paw.

It is a gift,
to see the world
through new eyes,
to see each thing
as though for the first time
and remember

that there are mysteries
yet to uncover,
and a world
yet to be explored.

And should we lose our way
among the new and strange
and all the myriad things
that beckon to us now,
then age will bring us home
while youth will keep us here,
securely fixed
among the newly found.

# I almost lived

I almost lived today.
I almost let my dreams take hold
and lead me to where I've never been.

I almost followed my instincts
and dropped the pretension
that this is all there is,
that the safe path
is the best path,
that the rewards of the well led,
comfortable life
far surpass those
of one
led slightly askew,
with risk and security out of balance
and thoughts of safety
held in abeyance
for the greater good.

I almost did the daring deed
and took the road less traveled
where chance and fate
lay intertwined along the way.

I almost,
should have
chosen differently
and moved away from acceptance,
moved away from a life of expectations
not my own,
to one
guided by my inner strength and purpose.

Curse the day and follow not the night

and all will be well.

Live in twilight and be not burned by the sun.

Walk in others' footsteps
and the road will be more smooth.

Risk all and be left with nothing.

Risk nothing and never gain the prize.

A conundrum,

A perplexity,

A mystery,

A choice.

I almost lived today.

# Come to me

It is the simple things
that keep me close to you.

A leaf,
twisting slowly in the wind.

A nest,
empty in a winter's dawn.

A smile,
from a stranger's heart.

I think of you
when I see these things.

I feel you in the smallest
and the largest things,
waiting for that hurried step,
the patient laugh,
the flashing eyes.

I see you always
just a turn away,
a glimpse,
a glance,
an almost there,
a maddening silent game
of "Here I am,
if only you can catch me."

And catch you I do
here within my heart
though I may find you
nowhere else.

Yet I see you
everywhere.

Feel you
in the slightest breeze.

Hear you
in the sweetest calls of birds
upon the midnight air.

You are the sum of all I am
and all I shall ever be
for it is you who leads me
through my every task,
my smallest deed,
and my mightiest accomplishment.

Is the world less sweet
for your absence?
No.
But you did make it your own
and in the blooming bud
I see the essence
that abides.

Come to me in dreams
and guide my sleep
that I may rest with you.

Come to me awake
that I may live in memory
and in fact.

Come to me in heart
that mine may beat again
and leave its cage of sorrow.

Bring me joy
in all its bright felt splendor,
pain
in all its darkest depths,
laughter
to make the world forget its sorrows,
tears
to wash away the wounds of life,
hate
of endings past renewing,
and love
that births all things anew.

But come to me.

## A Name

Sweet
would the words of wisdom be
had I but ears to hear them.

What is a name?
A thousand things
that move us to be
other than we are
if we change it.

Yet if we do,
can we transform our very nature
to be more,
or less,
than what we were before?

We may change our clothes
but we remain,
within,
regardless of the wrapping.

Can we flee to safety
within the confines of a name?
What we would not reveal of ourselves,
would we freely do as another?

Can we trust our self as another?
For there is a price that must be paid
if we seek to hide so.

If I were to say,
"You there,
tell me who I am.",
some would laugh and say,

"You are this name
or that name."
Still others would declare,
"Why you are this rank
or that title",
and all would be correct.

I am surely these
yet they are not me.
Though the name and title suit the clothes,
neither describes the self within.

If I bleed,
it is not a name
from which the blood flows.

If tears should bless this face
that bears the label of my self,
a name does not staunch the flow.

Whence does being come?
What import does a title bring
that we should judge it so?

It is not the name
that brings forth joy
or shares the love
that joins all things.

A name.
As I would know my self,
I have no need of one.

But you must frame me
in your world,
in its paths and ways,
to bind me to your purpose.

You use a name
to keep me so.

But you are not alone in this.
The world itself
conspires to make it so.

Without a name
I would be free,
of form,
of shape,
of fate
that holds me in its firm, unyielding grip
'til it be done with me.

A name.
As you would have it so,
I am.
Call me
and my form responds.

Still, I shape my self without it
and move my fate
to meet the dawn
of days unseen.

The price for such must be paid.
But not yet.
Not yet.
It is in the hour of the telling
that coin must be purchased for the bill
and spent when ending must be made.

A name.
Use it 'til the telling be complete.
Then choose anew,
that world shall know

and to its bosom clasp this wandering soul
lest it drift unseen among you.

A name.
As I make it mine,
it will do,
for now.
For the telling must unfold
and to its chosen ending go.
And so
I wear
a name.

# At first sight

She will know him when she sees him,
the one to make things right,
to end the lonely days
and fill the empty nights.
He will be the constant companion of her heart
and she will feel him
there,
just there,
ever present,
a part of her very essence.

She will measure him with a glance,
judge him by a touch,
love him instinctively
in that first instant of greeting,
where sight
and touch
and instinct
meld into a knowledge,
melt into a hunger,
a longing
deeply felt and ever present.

She had forgotten the feeling,
had abandoned consideration
that this emptiness
was anything but her fate,
was anything other than
a permanent state of being,
the hope of anything else
thought long extinguished.

Unexpected,
yet he will be there,

a surprise,
a joy,
a question and an answer
for her secret fears and dreams.

He will fill her senses
and awaken deep desire
and fit,
simply fit
as though a key long lost was found,
a door once locked was opened
and the future made possible once again.

Yes, she will know him when she sees him,
but will he know her?

Will he take her in his arms
and let shared passion
melt them into one,
one flame,
one heart,
one thought,
with all else forgot
in the blur of scent
and touch
and need
now joined in equal measure by his own?

Will his love be unreserved,
given freely,
a match to newfound joy
and unbound hope?

And if not,
she will bind him
with ploys and sweet inducements
and direct contention with his better self

until the two become one
and sated, rest entwined
with future bright within.

For who can say
that he did not love her at first sight
once his eyes were opened
and he saw her truly
as she saw him
in that first instant of greeting
when destiny was made manifest
in that first hello,
and all became possible
once more.

# A Word

A word.

It comes upon me suddenly
to strike my thoughts
with fierce delight
and thus distract me so.

Stop!
Write now!
Do not delay
or else this word
will slip away
to somewhere else this day.

Pause not,
but write until
the pen should stop
and this and other words
upon the page have dropped.

Look not for meaning
or for depth
but let them blithely come
all unconcerned with tasks ahead
amidst the daily scrum.

They do not stop
for you or me
but swiftly move away.
That they should pause and linger here
proves this a happy day.

Woe to those
whose noise and play

through busy day
drowns out these wayward sprites.

They do not tarry,
over long,
if they should deign to stop,
to wait for frenzied minds to clear
and tasks for them to swap.

See, they flee,
gone far from here
and now away from me,
except for one
that flits and taunts,
unyielding to my pleas

that it should stay
a moment more,
a moment more I ask,
so I can truly capture it
and others that have passed.

But 'tis gone
and vanished now
as rapid as it came,
perhaps to bless another,
yet always to remain

a word.

## The Legend of the Fire Tree

Deep within the Winter
beyond the Threadbare Sea
the Fire Tree stands as symbol
of the life that's yet to be.

The Fire Tree blooms in Winter,
against all odds succeeds,
with bright red blooms of fire
to meet its snowy needs.

It stands there as a beacon,
a blazing patch of hope.
It grows along the eastern side
of the northern facing slope.

You cannot doubt its presence,
the red against the snow,
that moves just like a flame
when the Winter winds do blow.

No heat, no warmth, no comfort,
no solace does it bring
except as herald serving
of the oh so distant Spring.

And should the snow long tarry,
should Winter long remain,
then long will Fire Tree blossom,
long will the Fire Tree reign

'til at last the blossoms falter
replaced by reddish sheen
of leaves that serve as shelter
for the birds that sit and keen

in wonder at the marvel
of a tree 'midst Winter's white
that gives them home and shelter
'gainst the long, cold Winter's night.

And still a fortnight later
the Fire Tree shall bear
a harvest for the patient
of fruit both large and fair.

A miracle of nature
when fire fruit does fall
a fire feast for man and beast
a banquet there for all.

Deep within the Winter
beyond the Threadbare Sea
the Fire Tree stands as symbol
of the life that's yet to be.

# Bespoken

I am bespoken
but my heart belongs to me
to give as I would
between dawn and dusk
and in my dreams.

I am bound
by duty,
by commitment,
by the dictates of my heart
and the reason of my mind.

And if the wind should blow
shall I follow,
a seed
blown 'til it find ground to grow,
or stand,
a rock against it,
a tree bending to it,
a reed swaying gracefully
yet firmly fixed
to this one spot,
a landmark,
a fixture in others' worlds,
rooted and immovable?

And if a fire burns
do I feed it,
with my yearnings giving fuel
to all consuming blaze
that sweeps away the old
leaving fertile ground behind
ready for future possibilities?

Do I feed it not
leaving only embers
banked,
yet potent harbingers
of silent need?

Do I put it out
with tears of steel
forged through constant beating
'gainst the anvil of my heart?

Do I deny it burns
Yet welcome
The heat it brings?

Rooted,
swaying,
burning hot,
a fixture
and a rock,
denying,
starving,
forged,
though I knew it not.
I am of two worlds,
dream and awake,
thought and reality,
heart and present fact.

I am certain of my dreams.
I am constant in my thoughts.
I know where my heart lies.
It is the others that I am unsure of.

Wakeful reality,
full of fact,
does not bind my other half

yet keeps me here
as measure of its hold on me.

Will I find myself within my dreams,
only to lose myself in fact?

Will my mark be writ in wind
or in the sands of time?

Will I be as certain tomorrow
as I am now
of things held dear today?

All will change.

All will vanish,
and in a twinkling
will the world known now be gone,
replaced by other facts,
other duties,
other commitments,
other realities.

And if my dreams,
thoughts,
and heart
should follow
then who I am today
would be as memory and forgotten
save for wistful musing
'neath an autumn sky.

I am bespoken
but I am alive with hopes,
ever present though unmet,
and when all else shifts
I pray the hopes remain

fixed and firm
against the changing world
as guide through tempest
and through calm
to what lies beyond.

Dreams,
thought,
and heart
will take me where they will
and if they be one with hopes
then let fact mold itself to match
and make reality create a world
more suited to them
and to me.

# A Caged Bird

Inside this cage I sit
and watch the world go by
through bars that keep me safely here.

I am fed,
and drink my fill of water.

I am warm,
and fear not predator's approach.

I have companionship
with one like,
yet unlike myself
in understanding and in view
of this our cage and home.

I may unfurl my wings
and beat them 'gainst the air
for the sake of doing so,
but I may not fly
and sense the freedom
of the air and the wind.
The cage is far too small
for more than simple jumps
from here to there,
from perch to food
and back again.

It is idyllic,
save for lack of freedom
to be what I am,
to soar and fly as I am capable
except for this cage,
these bars that hold me so.

And yet I am free within this cage
to test the limits of its boundaries.

I may do as I please within these bars.

I may move.

I may eat.

I may sit.

I may drink.

I may watch the world without
in all its changing glory
and be thankful for the warmth
when it is cold;
Grateful for the dry
when it is wet;
Glad for the sustenance
when there is none without,
Out there,
beyond these plain and barren bars
that keep me guest and prisoner both
within the world as I know it.

I know no other life
and though I yearn
I am not equipped
for other than I have.

Open up the door and let me fly
and I will know not what to do;
How to live;
Where to go
to live a life of freedom

with no bars to hold me,
no cage to claim as home,
no place to rest
except where I halt at end of day.

Had I no cage,
would I build another
and call it nest to give me comfort
that I might have a place
to perch,
to roost,
among the bits of life gathered there?

I know my destiny,
here behind these bars,
here within my well-appointed nest.
I need not wonder what tomorrow brings.
It will find me here as I am now
until I am not.

I might be able,
if I tried,
to lift the door
and flee my home,
this cage.
But to what avail?

I would be hungry and afraid.
I would be wet
and moving towards uncertain fate.
I would be cold
with no shelter save what I could fashion
with my native wit.

But I would be free.

# The birth of the new world

It isn't far,
the distance from then to now,
a decision,
a choice,
an act,
to do or do not,
to stay or walk away,
to renew or destroy,
and everything changes.

One world ends
and another begins.

You cannot blame another
despite the number
of others standing near
or even with you.

You must bear responsibility
for being here,
now,
as you are
and no one
can carry that weight
for you.

Be guilty or happy
with the choice
that brings you here.
It is all the same.

You are still here
and no amount
of regret or joy

will move you back again
to where you were,
to how the world was
before you decided,
before you chose,
before you acted
and everything changed.

# Consequences

Hope and despair
are like strong drink,
much alike in their ability
to govern actions.
Decisions made
under their influence
are often regretted later.

Reason is often a casualty
as people shout,
anger speaks,
and emotions have their day.
But do not blindly follow
to where you would be led.

Do not believe the one
who tells you
there is only one way,
that the others are to blame,
and that all will be well
if only you trust,
if only you surrender
rights and freedoms
for the greater good.

And in the aftermath,
when victory is declared
and today's foe
is seen as vanquished,
folk may not realize
what they have lost,
may not see
what has slipped away
in the rush to judgment,

in their haste to blame others
for the state of things,
for the loss of a way of life
that cannot be reclaimed.

What can be done to one
can be done to all.

If you can suppress one vote,
you can suppress all votes.

If you can deny a single right,
you can deny all rights.

If you can restrict one choice,
you can restrict others.

If you elevate
one set of beliefs,
then all others are
dismissed as unworthy,
as untrue,
and undeserving of protection
and everyone is affected
in small ways
or in large.

If you curtail the freedom of one
to speak freely
without fear of punishment
or retribution,
you have curtailed all speech.

If you can imprison one
without due process,
then all are at risk.

If you can kill any
without consequence,
then no one is safe.

If the rule of law
only favors some,
it may not favor you
tomorrow
and will not serve
as protector
or friend
for those unable to afford more.

We are all connected.
The rights of your neighbors
are your rights.

Strip them of theirs
in fear,
or anger,
or religious belief,
or righteous indignation,
and you diminish your own,
paving the way
for further intolerance,
greater persecution,
and distrust.

Anger, fear, and hate
are powerful weapons,
tremendous motivators,
but they seldom foster greater freedom,
seldom respect the rights
of those they are directed against,
seldom pay heed
to principles under the law
of equal rights,

justice,
and social liberties.

It is easy to blame
and easy to forget
that once the dust has settled
and trust has been misplaced
that rights and freedoms
given up
or taken
will not easily be restored.

It is easy to forget
that actions
taken under the influence
have consequences.

# Corruption

Corruption is insidious.

It begins with the first threat
and the acquiescence
in the face of
loss of liberty,
of business,
of public funds.

It begins with a handshake,
a smile,
a nod,
a denial of the truth,
and the embrace
of a convenient fib
that let's you sleep at night
when your soul screams
that this is wrong,
that you should say no,
that principles matter,
and that no job,
no work,
no amount of money
is that important.

But then you stop and think,
"If I don't make the deal
someone else will",
that it doesn't really matter
that you have to kiss
this guy's ass
to seal the deal,
that at least
you'll be rich

and your folks
will have jobs.

And so it begins
with a browbeating,
a threat,
an example made
here and there
until they all fall in line
and dance to the leader's tune.

Checks and balances only work
if someone cares enough
to pay attention to what occurs
right in front of them.
And once the balance is lost
and check unused
the slide becomes immediate
and pronounced.

Facts become unimportant.
Only the leader's words,
and those of his friends,
have merit,
have strength
and are worth listening to
since only his friends will prosper
and only they
can open the right doors
for someone more interested
in wealth than right,
in position
more than fact,
in survival
more than the common good.

Once corruption has a foothold,

it destroys institutions
with a casual flick of ill intent
leaving them as just enforcers
of the leader's will,
protectors of his friends' ambitions,
and a shield to all misdeeds
done in the leader's name.

Forget rights,
for they are what
they let you have.

Forget freedom,
for you will be free
to do as you are told.

Forget justice,
for it will serve
only the inner circle
while all else
wait in vain.

Forget speech.
Think three times before speaking
then think again
for your words
will be used against you
in the court of ill opinion.

Corruption.
Once it begins
there is no end
if it gains a foothold.

It creeps into
the very fabric of life
until one cannot cut it out

without remaking the garment.

It undermines the system
and rots it from within
with every decision
made with thought of payoff
until graft is all there is,
the people's voice is stilled,
and all hope vanquished
by the friends of friends
and their friends.

Corruption is insidious.

# One last hope

They were drowning
and so they grabbed
at anything
that might give them
a chance at safety,
of surviving the here and now
and providing hope
for any sort of tomorrow.

And so they grabbed the rope
and never saw the noose,
grasped for hope
and never saw the lie
or if they did
looked past it
to the slender chance
that even a noose might bring.

For though it be a noose,
it was not that today.
Today it was a lifeline
to the boat,
for there must be a boat,
from whence it came.

If they could only
reach the boat
they would be safe
and today
that's all that mattered,
all that could matter
as the sea pulled
and beat at them
at every turn

threatening to drag them down.

The rope might be an illusion
tied to a foundering boat.
There might not even be a boat,
just the rope trailing
in the surging sea.

Or perhaps it was just a trick
to catch and bind them
as ballast or as worse
unless they should be found
worthy of a grander fate.

Yet there,
in the sea,
struggling against the water,
gasping for each breath,
none of that matters.

All that does
is the chance
that there is something more
than sea
at the other end of rope
and the hope
that that chance brings.

And so they grabbed.

# Future Tense

There are no jobs
on a dead planet
except for those lucky enough
to survive the dying of the world
breathing recycled air,
drinking water gleaned
from sweat and piss
and purified for human use
inside a dome of last resort.

For those lucky few
jobs are all they have.
They have jobs
but they cannot drink the water,
due to toxins it contains,
with what little
they can strain and filter
never enough to meet their needs.

They have work
but they cannot breathe the air
outside of their protective shell
for the air is poisoned
by lethal fumes permitted
as being beneficial to business.

And so they work
to scrape a living
and by doing so
survive in a Hell
made
by decisions
they cannot reverse,
by people

they had never known
in a world
that no longer existed.

But for the corporate owners,
industrial chiefs,
and the somehow other rich,
there is no need for climate
as long as there are profits.

There is no need to worry
about ravaged lands
and toxic aquifers
as long as they can afford
their special enclaves
where the air smells sweet
and the water runs free
from taps paid for
by the labor of those
whose hands bleed
from working
with steel and iron,
oil and coal,
and reclamation
of parts and materials
from places past saving.

And as for food,
that is a luxury
reserved for the wealthy
who can afford it
grown as it is
in small secluded tracts
of treated land
and unavailable to those
who toil to grow it.

For the rest
food comes from vats
of factory created protein
designed for mass consumption
by the poor who know no better.

After all,
they cannot miss
what they do not have
and such glop
sustains the body
if not the soul.

In repose,
they huddle
beneath the concrete sky
smelling the distinctive
metallic taint
of air recycled
and scrubbed
far beyond
what should be allowed
in normal circumstance.

But nothing is normal
for these folks
trapped in a world
not of their making,
caught in a scheme
benefiting others,
isolated from a world
no longer able
to renew its bounty
and sustain the very folks
relying on it
for their existence.

We are stewards of this world.
The planet will provide for us
if we care for it
and safeguard it
for our children
and all generations
yet to come.

But if we ruin it,
if we destroy its bounty
and the riches therein,
then our fate is sealed
and those yet to come
will linger on a dying world
huddled beneath that concrete sky,
surrounded by rising seas,
and barren lands,
trapped
with no recourse
or hope of escape.

Remember them,
those pitiful few,
those remnants
of a once proud
and prosperous folk,
as decisions are made
both great and small
that decide their future fate.

Remember,
and do not forget,
that there are no jobs
on a dead planet.

# Speak Truth to Power

Speaking truth to power
is a futile act.
Power will crush you
and grind you in the dirt
until only dust
and echoes of your truth
remain.

Speaking truth to power
is courageous
for from this act
do better futures come
if you are heard
and truth heeded.

Speaking truth to power
is a civic right
and duty
not to be ignored
or cast aside
in the face of threats,
in the midst of corruption,
and the presence of danger
or hope dies,
power governs all,
and truth is forgotten.

Speaking truth to power
is a desperate act
for it will not bring
fame or glory
to the one who speaks it
when wrong is all there is,
rights have been suppressed,

and freedom fades
to only what power
will allow.

It is not easy.
It is not safe.
There is no reward
for speaking so.
Yet still we stand
in the face of tanks,
in the face of hatred,
in the face of lies,
against the slow erosion
of freedom
and the quick denial
of liberty
and of rights
through law no longer written
or enforced
for the common good.

It is a duty.
It is a sign of hope.
It is an act of desperation
to try and make today
the better place
we spoke of
yesterday.

It may not work.
It seldom does,
at first,
but if one does not speak,
no one speaks.
If no one acts,
then nothing is achieved.

Speaking truth to power
is essential
for power unchecked
will serve only its own ends
despite what truth
and evidence
might lay bare before it.

Speak.
Rise up.
March to make tomorrow
a place where we will want to be,
a place where all
may live in freedom
and respect
for the rights of all,
not just the empowered few,
and power is restrained by law,
not the owner of it.

## An Autumn's Walk

A quiet country lane,
unchanged by time's swift course,
untouched and undisturbed
since last we passed this way,
lies there waiting
for tread of foot upon the path.

The dog with eagerness of play
does forge ahead
with freedom gained from leased release
to run and scatter leaves
from place where nature's hand
did set them in repose.

It is enough to see him play
as I cannot as I would want
for time has brought me to this place
when I am no longer as I was
and free to play in boundless spurts
of youthful joy across the meadowland.

But youthful still in mind and play
the dog does run and bark and bay
at wonders found by stone,
by brook,
in tree roots sheltered nooks
along this lane of newfound things
within our grasp and ken

where nature's gifts await
for eyes to see
and eager paws to dig,
and nose to sniff at unthought scents
upon the crisp, cool air

and under boughs of pine
dressed for winter's coming chill.

I follow,
slow upon the lane,
with footsteps in the dust of time
to mark my passage in this place,
comforted
that I see a sameness in this scene
of dog and man in nature's midst.

Calling with a whistle and a shout,
to rein my young friend in,
I turn and wander further down
this simple path among the trees
and pasture's peacefulness
towards turning just ahead.

For there is much to see for us
within this sheltered way
and sunlight yet to wander in
upon this autumn day
'til we've had our fill of trees,
and field,
and country lane.

And should the darkness find us thus,
quite heedless of the time,
we shall with cautious steps
retrace
to where we had begun,
to share our gathered memories,
beneath the waning sun.

The lane will wait
and safely guard the secrets we have shared,
until we next should come this way

and so disturb the long lain dust
and treasures stored in nature's trust,
until we next should come this way
again.

# All tomorrows

I heard your voice
and was lost,
held as one entranced
by the first sound of music.

One glance,
and I knew the meaning of beauty
with all else fading to insignificance.

One touch,
and I knew that nothing
could compare to this,
to this...

One dance,
and all existence
became this moment,
became your voice,
that glance,
your touch,
this dance,
and all tomorrows became today,
all my futures became now,
and forever was captured
here in your arms.

# Compulsion

Writers write
because they must.
They give no mind
to whether cow
or tree
be only witness
to their toil.

Their fevered minds
embrace the words
that launch assault upon them,
or knock gently
'gainst more worldly cares
for admittance.

Writers listen
for what is not there,
hear
the unspoken words,
capture for the nonce
a thought,
a dream,
a vision
others let pass by,
unnoticed,
unremarked,
unobserved
among all else that transpires.

Writers know
that the imperfect
is the mirror of the soul
but seek to capture it
as though reverse were true

and words
melt present flaws
as mist
before the sun.

Writers abhor the unfinished
yet know that all is so
until the final word is written,
knowing that it never is.

It is a game between them,
the writer and the words,
a dialogue,
a love affair,
a compulsion
that transcends the waiting world
and brings them to the brink of self,
of conscious knowing of the hidden truth.

In the end,
the words win
and cow
and tree
and writer
are the better for it.

Another time,
another place,
another may reflect on this
but not I,
not this day,
for the words call to me
and I must follow.

## Another You

I saw another you today,
the one at twenty three
with child at her knee
embraced in loving hug
and smothered kisses
given forth
with deep felt satisfaction.

I know it was not you,
it could not be,
for your life went a different way
and dreams of family
remained but dreams
unrealized
through the passing years.

But it was you,
there below,
within the gated park
where children played upon the slides
and parents watched,
unconcerned with more important things
for there were none than this,
for now.

I saw you,
warm and gentle,
smile
with loving grace upon the boy
and standing,
take his hand
to lead him off towards home.

I know it was not you

and yet it was
more than just a glimpse
at realized ghost
of hoped for future.

It was real,
with substance born
by beauty of the woman
and her child
there for me
and all to see
within the circle of that park,
within the shelter of their happiness,
under the shadow of my gaze
and present fact.

I saw another you today.

# The middle

Each end is a beginning.
Each beginning is an end.
Life is lived in the in-between,
the place where neither is known,
where fate
hangs on the balance of our decisions,
of our actions,
and our mistakes.

It is in the middle where the story is told,
where the end and its meaning,
if one is to be had,
are made,
where the pieces
are bound together into one whole
and life unfolds at measured pace
for all who care to see.

It is in the middle
that you will find meaning,
where you will find
the motivations of a lifetime,
those factors big and small
that shaped the way between.

The end may have importance
with its triumph or defeat
but there were a thousand smaller things
that led to this along the way,
that made the end
both possible and necessary
if the fates may be believed.

Each act,

each twist,
each turn
are significant,
markers of a path lived upon and forged
with every well-placed step upon the way.

And careless steps as they may be
as plans amount to naught
and other pleasures bind us
to the unseen line
from here to there and elsewhere,
all unknown.

It is uncertain,
in the middle,
what the end will be
and perhaps this is unimportant
as we live the days between.

For if we knew,
would we live them less,
choose differently,
be other than we are?
For if we are choice,
would one choice make us different,
the way more simple,
and the end less sure?

And if it would,
would we be more circumspect?
Would we change?
Would we chose to live differently
and hide from certain fate
traced from our actions,
found within our tasks,
present in our trials,
and existing

even in those perfect moments
of hope and success?

We live in the middle,
with its mix of happiness and sorrow,
adversity and opportunity,
tragedy and sublime bliss,
and each marks the start or finish
of a chance,
an expectation,
misfortune,
accomplishment,
or understanding.

Each end is a beginning
and each beginning is an end.
But we never know which it is,
here in the middle,
until it is too late,
the world has turned,
and all is as it will be.

# A wondrous thing

To have been loved is a wondrous thing.
To know that there is one person
with whom all things are possible,
with whom no topic is off limits,
with whom the bond is such
that distance is no barrier to togetherness.

It does not come often,
this connection,
this link,
this bond,
perhaps once in every lifetime.
And when it does
there is no doubt
that this is the one thing
you can be sure of,
that fills the empty spaces
and makes all else right.

Peace and certainty,
happiness and comfort,
two souls touching,
blending as if one,
and having once known this
nothing will ever match it.

To have surrendered oneself
with no thought of gain or loss,
unreservedly,
with full abandonment of rhyme and reason,
to have yearned when there is no cause
save one,
to have had no purpose
but to exist in the fullness of joy,

this,
this is love
which absence is most strongly felt
when we know it not.

And if it should not stay,
if we find ourselves again alone,
the knowledge that love was not a dream,
that it was and is still true,
that what once was can be again,
keeps us whole,
keeps us searching for the other half
though we may never again find it
in quite the same way
with quite the same fit.

And if by chance it does,
if we are surprised again
by the newness of it all,
if we find our inner self
mirrored in the heart of one
beyond all expectation,
beyond all reason,
beyond all doubt,
with all our faults and flaws forgot,
our blemishes erased,
and weakness turned to strength,
then our future is assured,
our past is made manifest,
and our today become complete.

## A veteran's salute

I was a soldier once
but that was another life.
I stood proudly under arms
to serve in time of strife.
I am no longer strong of arm,
no longer fleet of foot,
but I remember all that served
and just how tall they stood.

They did not serve for glory
for really there is none
in the fury of the battle
and the struggle lost or won.
They did not serve for pay
for the pay was not that great
and none can spend their earnings
from the downward side of fate.

They gave their all for country
and for their fellow man
across the fields of Flanders,
and Tunisian burning sands,
through jungles deep in Burma
and those of Vietnam
across Iraqi deserts
and in Afghanistan.

They served for many reasons
and one of them was pride
for our country and its people
where liberty abides.
They served for common future,
to preserve what had been won
by all who came before them,

all the daughters and the sons

who kept the air above us
safe and truly free
or sailed in mighty warships
across disputed seas
or moved into the battle
'cross deadly island sands
or fought the bitter enemy
in combat hand to hand.

How gallant all, how brave and true,
all worthy to the core
who served to preserve freedom
during peacetime and in war.
They did not shirk their duty.
They answered true and brave
to serve beneath the hallowed flag
that still above us waves.

I was a soldier once
stood proudly under arms
and I remember all who served
and kept us safe from harm.
I cannot thank them properly
for standing strong and tall
but I honor each and every one
for answering the call.

## This face

I have grown into this face.
It somehow never seemed
quite right before.

The angles.
the slopes,
the various shapes and curves
never seemed to go together
in a way that made sense,
where all the parts fit together,
and looked
like they were meant to be there
and not just a collection
of odds and ends thrown together
at the whim of some lesser god
still practicing at assembling
human anatomy.

It never seemed to work,
this face.
It never quite made sense
in the way that others did.
It wasn't distinguished,
overly handsome,
or even of a scholarly mien.

It just was,
a mismatched combination
of features that just never fit,
never merged,
never came together
in a satisfying way
to present to the world
the me I wanted it to see.

Bold,
Confident,
Caring,
Complete,
and not someone
still finding their footing,
never fully trusting
the permanence of the rug
having had it pulled
oh so firmly away
on so many occasions before.

This face seemed fitted
for the background,
blending with the scenery
to be never truly seen,
a blur behind the important stuff,
never noticed except in absence
and even then as something sensed
instead of missed along the way.

I don't know why.
It always seemed strange to me
that it should be this way.
Perhaps it never was so.
Perhaps I only saw it thus.
Perhaps it only lacked an acknowledgement
and a kind of certitude
somehow missing before.

My face looks no different.
The same old shapes remain
with angles sharp
and pieces thrown in such a way
that... well you know.

But somehow today they fit,

they match,
they look good in a way
they just didn't before,
complete,
finished,
an honest face
reflecting hope
at what could yet be
and acceptance of what will not.

All is the same
and yet all is different
for I have grown into
this face.

# Changeling

I love you not for what you do,
(though that would be enough
should I but speak the truth),
but rather for what you do to me.

With you here
I see a world of chance
and possibility,
where hope and happiness
exist in fact and not in dreams,
where all that can be – is
and contentment
rests as soft upon my brow
as air upon the very ground.

I have lost all trace of sadness,
forgotten all sense of woe,
and found myself bereft of sorrow.
Where once there were a thousand paths
with equal claim to reach tomorrow,
there is but one
and every waking thought does take me there.

I am no more alone
and lost within myself
but now am guided
by the very notion of your love
that stirs my soul
and wakes my heart from slumber.

I do not recognize myself.
With you,
I am a new man,
and I am the better for it.

# Tom Bailey

Tom Bailey was an addled boy,
'twas said not fully sane,
whose father, cruel and hard at heart,
still often spared the cane,
and used the rod instead
to beat his wayward son,
for the awful, naughty things
his addled boy had done.

Tom Bailey grew to be quite swift
beneath the summer sun,
so now when father chose the rod
away the boy would run
down to the golden beach
where he would often play.
There beyond his father's reach
the happy boy would stay.

Was not an addled boy our Tom.
Was smart as you and me
and once beyond his father's reach
a wise man came to be.
He scavenged for the books
that others threw away
and soon amassed great knowledge
as though he schooled all day.

He'd sit there in the courthouse yard,
debate the learnéd men,
and once they finally let him in
he never left again.
Once there he studied hard
and learned the common law
to ensure justice for all folk

before the Bar he swore.

Tom became a learnéd lawyer.
His father was a thief.
Tom served the poor and rich alike.
His father sought gold leaf.
Tom worked hard in the day.
His father in the night.
And so the two would never meet
unless by chance they might.

While standing his turn in the court,
it gave Tom much relief
to see his father standing there
accused and judged as thief.
With sentence handed down
to punish for his crimes,
he saw his father sent to jail
to serve allotted time.

And thus the simple addled boy
became a learnéd man
who saw his father's wrongful ways
become but shattered plans.
But as a good son might
he paid his father's fine.
It gave Tom right to visit him
in jail from time to time.

"It serves you right you awful wretch
for you to come so low
but now you'll pay for every time
you hit me with a blow
for some imagined wrong,
for some imagined deed,
and here you'll stay until your frame
does feed the hungry weeds."

The moral of this simple tale,
if one is said to be,
is that a simple addled boy
may never simply be,
that justice comes to those
who strive to make it so
and those who cruelly treat their kin
will reap what they do sow.

# Consumed

Our eyes are black holes.
Whatever enters there
is carried far below
beyond the reach
of any who might seek
to bring it back.

It is
internalized,
compressed,
smashed,
rendered
into constituent bits,
consigned
to swirl forever
within that darkness.

But ever so often
a bit escapes,
rising unbidden
to the surface of our minds,
briefly,
oh so briefly,
'til it is squashed
and pushed
and squeezed
into the darkness yet again.

For to do otherwise
would be to release it,
and others,
to our outer selves
where their mass
would weigh us down

until,
in just a flash,
a simple blink of eyes,
we would be consumed.

## You could see it in his face

You could see it in his face,
the disappointment,
the bitterness,
the anger,
that someone else
stood there in his stead.

He had put
his heart and soul
into this.

He had willed it to be,
bringing it to life
with every long, fraught day
of hard-fought labor
and sleepless nights
of planning,
convincing,
and manipulation
of the final work
to shape it into what,
in his belief,
was a masterwork
deserving of this award.

He died inside,
sitting there,
enduring dread
and anticipation
as the name was announced
and someone,
but not he,
was anointed as the best
of those precious few

to be recognized for their work,
to be honored for their skill
above all the others
gathered with him
in that place.

"The work was its own reward",
that's what they all said
when questioned about their chances,
when queried as to their hopes
for recognition.

"It is an honor just to be nominated"
was the standard reply
meant to cover a complex mix
of anxiety,
pride,
ego,
and humility.

And it was for some
who had no real expectations
this night,
who were genuinely surprised
to find themselves
sitting there among the rest
perhaps more worthy
of such honor
and respect.

But not for him.
Not this night,
Not this time,
Not after all that work,
and sweat,
and sleepless nights
to bring the piece to pass,

that brought the thing to life,
and earned him his seat
here tonight.

No.
Tonight, it was all or nothing.
Either he won, or he lost
and no amount of platitudes
would fill the empty place
where this trophy
would have been
had his peers been smarter,
had they recognized,
at the last,
the sheer magnitude
and level
of his achievement.

And then the name,
not his,
clearly not his,
and he had to sit,
drowning in his bitterness,
swallowing his pride,
and listen to a speech
no one would remember
a month from now.

It was supposed to be his moment,
the crowning achievement
in a lifetime of good,
of great,
and almosts.
And the pain of having that
trampled beneath the altar
of another's glory
was almost too much to bear.

**You could see it in his face**

# Denial

We are all in denial
about one thing or another.

It is how we live our lives.

It is how we survive
from one day to the next
by ignoring this or that
about ourselves,
about others,
about the things
we ought to change
and would
if only we listened
to that little voice inside
saying "Don't",
"No",
"Oh God Yes",
"You Fool",
"You Idiot",
"What are you waiting for?",
and all the little feelings,
urges,
and intuitions
we will not touch.

For to do so
would change our lives
in ways unimaginable,
perhaps for the better,
but perhaps not
and so we live
the lives we have
and deny

that we could ever have another,
that another is even possible
until the moment is past,
the intuition fades,
and the opportunity is forgotten.

Doing otherwise
is to live another life,
to be someone else,
to abandon what we know
for the unknown
wherein danger lies,
truths are revealed,
and different denials beckon.

Because even then,
even with the changes,
even with the feelings followed,
the urge pursued,
the intuition acted on,
and the new lives lived,
we must still justify ourselves,
we must still believe
that we are where we should be,
that this is where we want to be,
regardless of everything
that says otherwise,
that shouts deep within
to do something different,
to be someplace
and someone else.

We are all in denial
about one thing or another.

It is how we live our lives.

## Early Frost

You are long gone from the wilding wood
to follow the western sun
and yet the trees remember
your passage based on one

moment by a waiting fence
unmarred by Autumn's touch
with all the world ablaze, adorned
unseen save by one such

as yourself who sat with idle scythe
the summer's mowing done
to mourn the sweet, swift passage
of all that life had brung

to this spot, this day, this moment,
and all that would come hence,
pondered, mourned in mid-day sun
beside that pasture fence.

But you were gone by evening's chill
and nighttime's misting rain
but trees' sure thought of early Frost
like idle scythe remain,

untouched by time's sure passage
bringing change to forest lane
the wilding wood still waits in vain
for visit once again

by the wandering gentle poet
with an ancient, restless soul
and a vision of the world apart
from strife and burden's toll.

The tufted flowers linger.
The butterfly still flits
across the verdant pasture
near where he used to sit

far from the road less traveled
far from the winter wood
far from the stone wall fences
where he and neighbor stood.

I shall not long here tarry
'neath the pale October sun
for early Frost has come and gone
with Winter soon begun.

# Escape

She insulted her husband
with the easy disdain
of long practice.

It wasn't that she hated him.
She loved him
or thought she did
and after forty some odd
years of marriage
perhaps
that was the same thing.

No,
she loved him
but she hated
what she had become,
hated what he was now,
and hated what they were together
after all this time.

So they traveled
to get away from themselves,
to change with the locale
much as you would change
a shirt or a dress.

It worked after a fashion.
They shifted to match the journey,
more continental here,
more urbane there,
changing to suit the scenery
and their companions.

They became exceptionally good at it

sliding as smoothly into roles
as ice into the cocktails
they liberally indulged in
in order to forget their other selves.
The problem was
they always brought
themselves along.

And after a while
they'd drift back
into the old familiar patterns,
the sniping,
the casual remark
that bit
and gnawed at old wounds
until they bled
and festered
and broke through the glad facade
they had so carefully crafted
to escape themselves.

In the end,
when the trip was over,
the journey done,
the facade stripped away
and pretense vanished
with the morning's sun,
they would sit and stare
and wonder at the whys
and ways of it all.

That they should stay together
when all instinct
cried to be apart.
That the old familiar pains,
worn into their very souls,
would be more comforting

than the chance of joy,
the possibility of happiness,
and the unknowns that lingered
just beyond their ken.

They almost remembered a time
when things were better,
almost.
But remembering
would require acknowledging
that things were not good now,
and that would never do.
It was far easier to make believe
that all was well
than to make it so.

So in the end
they ignored the past
and who they had become
until it really didn't matter anymore
as the insults came,
the sniping continued,
and time passed
as they waited within their allotted roles
'til their next escape
should free them.

# A Winter's Walk

This day plays with me,
one moment teasing,
almost pleading for me
to loose the strictures
of my winter clothes
and then the next
proving full,
with wind whipped chill,
that Winter still has claim
upon this place.

This path I take,
of gravel loosely packed,
will take me nowhere much
upon my walk
and yet it is enough
for day to play upon my yearning
for Spring to come.

Hillsides bear but touch of snow
upon their all unburdened brows
but still I feel
the bite of Winter in the air
and sense its frosty gaze
as I stroll along.

The stones beneath my feet complain
as stride leaves them here
with no recourse but time
to Winter's lingering touch.

And though I think to take one
to share this winter's walk,
I step ahead

and leave all to their fate,
fixed upon the path
'til future foot should kick them
on their way.

Once at summit's cap,
I pause among the trees
still shorn of their adornment.
No shelter here from bitter wind
that blows past empty land,
silent
except for branches' creak
and moaning
of the wind brushed limbs.

From here the path turns downward
towards the cabin far below
and I in haste depart
lest darkness catch me here
alone
and unawares of trail ahead.

Cabin's warmth does call to me,
but still I gaze across this frozen place
and promise to travel here again
on more favorable day.

Stooping,
I pick some gravel here
for memories to stay
bright and clear
lest I forget the hillside
and its wintry chill.

And thus fortified for memory's sake
I walk again with careful pace
along the darkening way

**to cabin's rest below.**

# By the time I leave

By the time I leave,
no one here will know me.

Oh they will think they do,
children,
neighbors,
loves,
acquaintances,
perhaps even a friend or two...
but no one will.

How could they?
I have kept a careful face to the world
seemingly unaffected
by the highs
and lows
of daily life.

I have kept myself apart
even while sharing all I am
in unobserved ways
between the then and now.

Each has seen what they wanted,
had what they required of me,
but none have known me.

None has known the joy
and sadness
that I have borne.

None can know of the choices
left lying in the dust,
of decisions unmade,

things undone,
of lives unlived
for the sake of others,
for the sake of a greater good
I would never share.

It is ever so,
that those who know you best
know you least,
for you are but
a figment of their desires,
framed by their needs,
and made whole
by their wish for constancy
and a world made safe
by the rock
to rest their fears upon.

Shhh.
Don't interrupt.
I know you believe
that I am wrong,
that all here know me
by my words,
by my deeds,
by the life I have led
that has brought me here.

You are mistaken.
For what I am,
who I am,
where I am
is as much
from what I did not do
as from what I did,
from the words unwritten
or unspoken

as from those read
or heard,
by those lives unlived
as by the one followed
to this place and time.

All my life
I have stood upon the precipice,
arms outstretched
and shouting to the wind
with no one there to hear.

I do not regret it.
The wind was always there
when you were not
and words blown here and there
may yet find a home
with those
who will think they know me
through their meaning.

It may be enough…
perhaps…
but they will know me less than you
and you at least
walked with me,
talked with me,
and laughed and cried with me
at the absurdity of it all,
seeing much
but understanding little.

Think on your own lives,
on how little
those who know you
really know you
and you will begin to understand

how,
by the time I leave,
no one here will know me.

# But one thing

If I had only one thing,
a single thing
in all the moments
held within the span of life,
to remember,
to cherish
in the darkness
as the embers
flared,
flickered,
and then died,
it would be
the day we met
there
beneath the autumn sky.

Oh there were other times,
other moments
of contentment,
of adventure,
of bliss.
But this one,
this one was the one
that made us who we were
and what we would become.

And had I the chance
to change it
I would not
for it was the end
of everything I knew
and the beginning
of every possibility
yet to be.

It is this single moment
that I would linger o'er,
as a lifetime's worth of moments
vanished in the gathering dark,
and I would stay within its span
as season turned more cold
beneath a sun still kind
and warm in generosity.

I cannot now recall
the words we shared
though they were enough
to bind our hearts together
with hopes
of what we would become.

But I do recall
that this was the moment,
the single instant,
where life began
and we started
the complex weave
where two became one
bound by joy,
by happiness,
by Love.

It was not easy.
It was not smooth
and threads were cut
and rewoven along the way
until the pattern became lost
in the meandering of life.

But here,
in this moment,
the weave was new,

the pattern fresh and bright,
as life lay full before us
and we were eager
to be on our way
together.

And so
if I had but one thing
to light the darkness
and keep me warm therein
it would be this,
the memory of autumn sky
and you.

# A path beneath the river

Runs a path beneath the river,
through the darkness that awaits,
that leads us from our bondage,
in the world of lies and hate.

There's a light left in a window
to guide us safely home
though the storm
be fierce and threatening
in demanding we atone.

There is a voice
beyond our ken
that beckons to us all
with truth's uncommon whisper
filling silence with its call.

There is a place of rest and hope,
before the next event,
where we may pause to bind the wounds
and pound out armor's dents.

It is a time of comfort,
sheltered from our greatest woes,
when we may take some solace
in the absence of our foes.

'Til rested, we must gird ourselves
to take the path again
though it be a thousand years
that passed or merely ten.

And emerge once more to daylight,
soon the battle to renew,

in the flush of morning's promise
of the deeds that we shall do.

For so it has been promised,
through all time it shall be thus,
we shall remain in battle
'til these forms return to dust.

And then the pathway shall we take
to wait our sanctioned turn
until we can emerge again
and feel our life's blood burn.

And wreak our bloody havoc
or speak the words of peace
it shall be known to none of us
'til our waiting time does cease.

For so it has been promised,
'til our vow we have appeased,
'til the end be close upon us
and at last we are released.

# When next I wake

When I sleep
I dream of different lives,
of turning left
instead of right,
of choices made differently
and the same,
of hopes fulfilled
or as often dashed
by fortune
or by circumstance.

I live each fully,
embracing friendship
and heartbreak
in their turn
with joy and sorrow
close companions on the way,
shaping,
but not determining,
the journey.

As I dream,
I recognize myself
in these most different folk,
all strangers to my waking self,
all intimately known
within my slumber
as I slip
between the thens and nows
within each moment
spent as them.

But soon,
too soon it seems at times,

I wake
and rid my eyes
of lingering sleep
to venture full into this life.

But even as I do,
I ponder if this
is but a longish dream,
to vanish with the rest at morning,
and with that thought
wonder
at who I will find myself to be
when next I wake.

## As Seen Through Amber

Everything changes.
The world is not the same today
as it was yesterday
or as it will be tomorrow.
Our memories of today
will fade,
will dim,
will vanish with us
into a certain future
where uncertainty reigns
and random chance
is as much a fact
as fated possibility.

But given this,
the past is still immutable.
Our actions,
thoughts and deeds,
are fixed in time,
like a fly in amber trapped,
for all to see
if light and opportunity
should find us thus exposed.

We cannot change them.
They are past our strength to move,
to change in our present state
and not 'til time itself
is bent to our demands
could we undo,
could we alter,
could we change
the actions thus encased.

Unlike the fly
we can still move.
We can change
the nature of our circumstance.
And though we are known by past,
it is our future that defines us
that marks us not as we are
but as we shall be
when time at last completes its grip
and has us in its firm embrace,
held fast within its span.

We are not bound
yet.
We are still free to move,
to act,
to think,
to change,
if we but choose to.

Everything changes
but the nature of change itself.
And even once encased
we change as others change their view,
shift their perceptions
and their thoughts of us.

Yet we ourselves will be stuck,
fixed as we were
in the moment of our undoing,
the sum of all our changes
measured only by the view
of those who knew us not,
who saw but did not understand,
or who understood but could not see
the reasons for it all,
the inner workings of the piece

that governed all the movement
leading to the view now seen
by those outside looking in
at the fly within the amber.

Everything changes
until it does not,
until change itself is trapped
and made captive to the whims of time,
and fate,
and chance occurrence
frozen in the instant of happenstance,
rendered solid and immutable.

Yet what is within
is but the appearance of the form.
It is shape without substance,
form without character,
beauty without being,
outline without content
without the drive to be,
unable to exist
independent of the view from without.

In the end
we will be a mystery,
like the fly in amber,
unknown save for what can be seen
through the medium of our fixing.
Time will obscure all else
denying those who look
any real satisfaction to their curiosity.

But not yet,
not yet.
Although the amber beckons,
today I am still free of it.

I can still fly
with my reasons my own.
I can still be more than I am
and though someday I will be claimed
and made a curiosity to ages hence,
today,
I can still change.
Today,
I am still free.

# But one day more

If I had but one day more,
I would spend it with you.

Had I a thousand days
or even much, much more,
unknowing
I would spend them thoughtlessly
on matters great and small
according to my needs,
and will,
and driving ambition.

And if the next day
was the last
then still would I live
the same
until no more was left.
But knowing there was but one,
there would be
but one place for me.

So many things to see and do
and all important
in a life well lived.
But if there was
only one day,
one day to capture,
one day to hold close,
one day to remember
'gainst illusion of the endless night,
then it would be this,
here,
with you.

The place,
the time,
the season,
would be of little consequence
except for the doing of it.

For you have given all you were
to make me all I am.
And what I might gain
by doing one thing more
would pale beside your need
for that one day,
for memory's sake,
so that at day's end
you would know
that nothing,
nothing,
was more important to me.

And when morning found me gone,
with dreams of futures all forgot,
there would be no doubt
of my love,
of my need,
of my desire,
of my choice,
that given certain knowledge
that that day would be the last
there would be but one place
I would be.

That if I had but one day more,
I would spend it with you.

# Flood

There is nothing
running through my mind right now
but soon,
soon it will come,
and then it will be relentless.

The surge of words
crashing past the outer markers of my mind
to pass within and through
with no regard for mindful self
that struggles 'gainst the undertow
to crest the torrent
and observe the meaning within.

Slowly.
Move more slowly.
You pass too fast for me to grasp,
and see,
and copy here for future's sake.

And yet,
if I do not struggle
but let myself be carried forth,
I feel that I shall know the reason
ere long
for this sudden passage.

Like a flood there may be no reason
except that it has rained
and banks are overflowed
and lost within the rest.

But I shall look regardless,
and wonder

at the patterns left behind
in pools and puddles
filled with residue and debris,
as surge abates,
words ebb,
and my mind is mine once more,
safe within its verdant banks
between the pastures of eternity.

Grieco

## ABOUT THE AUTHOR

Born and raised in a small rural town, the author left to pursue higher education and a career which took him to different parts of the world. After a lifetime listening to the whisper of the wind, the burble of a brook, and the sound of songbirds all imparting their wisdom, he's returned to his roots, spending his days as a country gentleman, taking the time now and then to put some words on paper.

Find more from Pat at pat-grieco.com